Nursery Rhymes

A Collection
from Mother Goose

Introduction and Compilation
Copyright © 1994 by Random House Value Publishing, Inc.
All rights reserved

First published in 1994 by JellyBean Press,
distributed by
Random House Value Publishing, Inc.,
40 Engelhard Avenue,
Avenel, New Jersey 07001

Editorial supervision: Nina Rosenstein
Production supervision: Roméo Enriquez

Manufactured in the United States

Library of Congress Cataloging-in-Publication Data
Mother Goose.
Nursery rhymes from Mother Goose / illustrated by Ella Dolbear Lee
and Anne Anderson.
p. cm.
Summary: A selection of Mother Goose rhymes
illustrated by a variety of artists.
1. Nursery rhymes. 2. Children's poetry. [1. Nursery rhymes.]
I. Lee, Ella Dolbear, ill. II. Anderson, Anne, ill. III. Title.
PZ8.3.M85 1994
398.8—dc20
94-11973
CIP
AC

ISBN: 0-517-11857-2

8 7 6 5 4 3 2

Nursery Rhymes

A Collection from Mother Goose

Edited by Glorya Hale
Designed by Liz Trovato

JellyBean Press
New York • Avenel

CONTENTS

INTRODUCTION

Whimsical and musical, nonsensical and charming, nursery rhymes have been enjoyed, memorized, and recited by children for hundreds of years. A baby is mesmerized by the echoing rhythm and singsong sounds, without even understanding that the words have meaning. To the growing child who is gaining mastery of language, nursery rhymes entertain on several levels of sound and story. It doesn't matter in the least if some of the words are quaint or even obscure. Children are drawn to the repetition from verse to verse ("This is the house that Jack built...") and delight in the silly twists on everyday life—"There was an old woman who lived in a shoe...," "If all the world were apple pie...." And there is always the anticipation of the rhyme that will end each set of lines.

Nursery rhymes are often a child's first experience with humor and irony and with the joys of playing with words to make pleasing sounds and comical associations. Budding poets and humorists love to flex their imaginations and add their own inventive verses and parodies to their most familiar favorites.

All the Mother Goose poems in this book are linked in spirit, but they actually came from a variety of sources. We know that some of the rhymes originated in France, others in England, and still others are of Irish, Scottish, and American origin. But nobody knows for sure where the name Mother Goose came from or how this legendary figure became associated with these rhymes. It has been said, but not substantiated, that it all began in the early eighteenth century with Elizabeth Goose, an Englishwoman who moved to Boston, where her son-in-law published a book of the verses she recited to her grandchildren. He titled the book *Mother Goose's Melodies for Children* or *Songs for the Nursery*.

Through the years many anthologies of Mother Goose have been published. This delightful new collection, with charming illustrations by Anne Anderson and Ella Dolbear Lee, includes more than fifty of Mother Goose's wonderful rhymes. Most of them, like "Little Bo-Peep," "Mary Had a Little Lamb," and "Humpty-Dumpty," you will certainly remember from your own childhood. A few, which may be unfamiliar, will be fun to learn along with the child to whom you're reading.

No matter how "Mother Goose" got involved with these rhymes, or where they originated, these traditional verses link our past with our future as they entertain new generations of children and also serve to introduce them to the cadence and rhyme of poetry.

Old Mother Goose when
  She wanted to wander,
Would ride through the air
  On a very fine gander.

Mother Goose had a house,
  'Twas built in a wood,
Where an owl at the door
  For sentinel stood.

She had a son Jack,
  A plain-looking lad;
He was not very good
  Nor yet very bad.

She sent him to market,
  A live goose he bought.
"Here, Mother," says he,
  "It won't go for nought."

Jack's goose and her gander
  Grew very fond,
They'd both eat together
  or swim in one pond.

Jack found, one fine morning,
  As I have been told,
His goose had laid him
  An egg of pure gold.

Jack rode to his mother,
  The news for to tell;
She called him a good boy,
  And said it was well.

Jack sold his gold egg
  To a rascally knave,
Not half of its value
  To poor Jack he gave.

Then Jack went a-courting
  A lady so gay,
As fair as the lily
  And sweet as the May.

Jack's mother came in
   And caught the goose soon,
And mounting its back,
   Flew up to the moon.

Little Jack Horner sat in the corner,
Eating his Christmas pie.
He put in his thumb and pulled out a plum,
And said, "What a good boy am I!"

I had a little nut tree, nothing would it bear
But a silver nutmeg and a golden pear.
The King of Spain's daughter came to visit me,
And all was because of my little nut tree.
I skipped over water, I danced over sea,
And all the birds in the air couldn't catch me.

Little Tommy Tucker
  Sings for his supper,
What shall we give him?
  Brown bread and butter.
How shall he cut it
  Without e'er a knife?
How shall he marry
  Without e'er a wife?

Little Boy Blue, come blow your horn,
The sheep's in the meadow, the cow's in the corn.
Where is the little boy who looks after the sheep?
He's under the haystack, fast asleep.

Jack Sprat could eat no fat

His wife could eat no lean

And so, betwixt them both you see,
They lick'd the platter clean.

Hickory dickory dock,
The mouse ran up the clock.
The clock struck one,
The mouse ran down,
Hickory dickory dock.

This little pig
went to market.

This little pig
stayed at home.

This little pig
had a bit of meat.

This little pig
had none!

This little pig
went . . .

Wee—Wee
Wee—Wee

All the way home.

Polly, put the kettle on,
Polly, put the kettle on,
Polly, put the kettle on,
And let's drink tea.

Sukey, take it off again,
Sukey, take it off again,
Sukey, take it off again,
They've all gone away.

I love little pussy
Her coat is so warm,
And if I don't hurt her
She'll do me no harm.
I won't pull her tail,
Nor drive her away,
And pussy and I
Very gently will play.

THERE WAS AN OLD WOMAN WHO LIVED IN A SHOE.

There was an old woman
Who lived in a shoe;
She had so many children
She didn't know what to do.

So she gave them some broth
With a piece of bread;
Then kissed them all gently
And put them to bed.

The man in the moon   He went by the South,
Came tumbling down,   And he burnt his mouth
And asked the way to Norwich.   With eating cold pease porridge.

Mary had a little lamb,
  Its fleece was white as snow;
And everywhere that Mary went
  The lamb was sure to go.

It followed her to school one day—
  It was against the rule—
And made the children laugh and play
  To see a lamb at school.

And so the teacher turned him out,
  But still he lingered near,
And waited patiently about
  Till Mary did appear.

And then he ran to her, and laid
  His head upon her arm
As if he said, "I'm not afraid,
  You'll shield me from all harm."

"What makes the lamb love Mary so?"
  The eager children cry.
"Why, Mary loves the lamb, you know,"
  The teacher did reply.

Once I saw a little bird
  Come hop, hop, hop.
So I cried, "Little bird,
  Will you stop, stop, stop?"
And was going to the window
  To say, "How do you do?
But he shook his little tail,
  And away he flew.

Simple Simon met a pieman
   Going to the fair.
Says Simple Simon to the pieman,
   "Let me taste your ware."

Says the pieman to Simple Simon,
   "Show me first your penny,"
Says Simple Simon to the pieman,
   "Indeed I have not any."

OLD KING COLE

Old King Cole was a merry old soul,
And a merry old soul was he.
He called for his pipe,
And he called for his bowl,
And he called for his fiddlers three.

Now, every fiddler, he had a fine fiddle,
And a very fine fiddle had he.
"Tweedle-deedle-dee," went the fiddlers.
  Oh, there's none so rare,
  As can compare
  With King Cole
    and his fiddlers three.

SING A SONG O' SIXPENCE

Sing a song of sixpence,
  A pocket full of rye;
Four-and-twenty blackbirds
  Baked in a pie.

When the pie was opened
  The birds began to sing;
Wasn't that a dainty dish
  To set before a king?

The king was in his counting-house,
Counting out his money;

The queen was in the parlor,
Eating bread and honey;

The maid was in the garden,
Hanging out the clothes;
When down flew a blackbird
And snapped at her nose.

Little Miss Muffet sat on a tuffet
Eating her curds and whey.

There came a great spider,
Who sat down beside her,
And frightened Miss Muffet away.

The North Wind doth blow,
   And we shall have snow,
And what will poor Robin do then,
                  Poor thing!

He will sit in the barn,
   To keep himself warm,
And hide his head under his wing,
                  Poor thing!

See-saw, Margery Daw,
    Jenny shall have a new master,
She shall have but a penny a day,
    Because she can't work any faster.

See-saw, Margery Daw,
    Jacky shall have a new master,
He must have but a penny a day,
    Because he can't work any faster.

Goosie, goosie, gander
   Where do you wander?
Upstairs and downstairs
   And in my lady's chamber.

If all the world were apple pie,
If all the seas were ink,
If all the trees were bread and cheese
What would we do for drink?

TOM HE WAS A PIPER'S SON

Tom he was a
 piper's son,
He learned to play
 when he was young,
But the only tune that
 He could play
Was "Over the hills
 and far away."

Now Tom with his pipe
 made such a noise
That he pleased both
 the girls and boys,
And they all stopped to
 hear him play
"Over the hills and
 far away."

Tom with his pipe did play
   with such skill,
That those who heard him
   could never keep still;
Whenever they heard him
   they began to dance
Even pigs on their hind legs
   would after him prance.

As Dolly was milking her
   cow one day,
Tom took out his pipe and
   began to play;
So Doll and the cow danced
   "the Cheshire round,"
Till the pail was broke, and
   the milk ran on the ground.

He met old Dame Trot with
a basket of eggs;
He used his pipe, and she
used her legs.

She danced about till the
eggs were all broke;
She began to fret, but he
laughed at the joke.

Peter, Peter, pumpkin-eater
Had a wife and couldn't keep her,
He put her in a pumpkin shell,
And there he kept her very well.

Peter, Peter, pumpkin-eater,
Had another and didn't love her.
Peter learned to read and spell,
And then he loved her very well.

RIDE A COCK HORSE

Ride a cock horse
   to Banbury Cross
To see a fine lady
   on a white horse.
With rings on her fingers
   and bells on her toes,
She shall have music
   wherever she goes.

Mary, Mary, quite contrary,
How does your garden grow?
With cockle shells and silver bells
And pretty maids all in a row.

Bow-wow,
    says the dog;

Meow, meow,
    says the cat;

Grunt, grunt,
    says the pig;

Squeak, squeak,
    says the rat;

Who, who,
    says the owl;

Caw, caw,
    says the crow;

Quack, quack,
    says the duck,

And Moo,
    says the cow.

Hark! Hark! The dogs do bark
The beggars are come to town.
Some in rags, and some in tags
And one in a velvet gown.

Hey! diddle diddle,
    the cat and the fiddle
The cow jumped over the moon.

The little dog laughed
    to see such sport,
And the dish ran away with the spoon.

THE HOUSE THAT JACK BUILT

This is the house
that Jack built.

This is the malt
That lay in the house
  that Jack built.

This is the rat
That ate the malt
That lay in the house
  that Jack built.

This is the cat
That killed the rat
That ate the malt
That lay in the house
  that Jack built.

This is the dog
That worried the cat
That killed the rat
That ate the malt
That lay in the house
    that Jack built.

This is the cow
    with the crumpled horn
That tossed the dog
That worried the cat
That killed the rat
That ate the malt
That lay in the house
    that Jack built.

This is the maiden,
  all forlorn,
That milked the cow
  with the crumpled horn
That tossed the dog
That worried the cat
That killed the rat
That ate the malt
That lay in the house
  that Jack built.

This is the man
  all tattered and torn
That kissed the maiden,
  all forlorn.
That milked the cow
  with the crumpled horn
That tossed the dog
That worried the cat
That killed the rat
That ate the malt
That lay in the house
  that Jack built.

Georgie Porgie pudding and pie
Kissed the girls and made them cry,

When the boys came out to play
Georgie Porgie ran away.

Baa, baa, black sheep,
  have you any wool?
Yes sir, yes sir —
  three bags full:
One for the master,
  one for the dame,
And one for the little boy
  that lives in our lane.

Bobby Shaftoe's gone to sea,
Silver buckles on his knee;
He'll come back and marry me,
Bonny Bobby Shaftoe!

Bobby Shaftoe's young and fair
Combing down his yellow hair,
He's my love for evermore,
Bonny Bobby Shaftoe.

LITTLE BO-PEEP

Little Bo-Peep has lost her sheep,
   And doesn't know where to find them;
Let them alone and they'll come home,
   And bring their tails behind them.

Little Bo-Peep fell fast asleep,
   And dreamt she heard them bleating;
But when she awoke she found it a joke,
   For still they all were fleeting.

Then up she took her little crook,
   Determined for to find them;
She found them indeed,
   But it made her heart bleed,
For they'd left their tails behind them.

It happened one day, as Bo-Peep did stray
   Unto a meadow near by,
There she spied their tails, side by side,
   All hung on a tree to dry.

Then she heaved a sigh, and wiped her eye,
   And ran over hill and dale-o,
And tried what she could,
   As a shepherdess should,
To tack to each sheep its tail-o.

Pat-a-cake, pat-a-cake, baker's man!
Bake me a cake as fast as you can.
Prick it, and pat it, and mark it with T,
And put it in the oven for Tommy and me.

Baby, baby, bunting,
Daddy's gone a hunting.
To fetch a little bunny skin
To wrap baby bunting in.

The Queen of Hearts
She made some tarts,
All on a summer's day.

The Knave of Hearts
He stole those tarts,
And took them clean away.

The King of Hearts
Called for the tarts,
And beat the Knave full sore.

The Knave of Hearts
Brought back the tarts,
And vowed he'd steal no more.

Ding, dong, bell,
Pussy's in the well.

Who put her in?
Little Johnny Green.
Who pulled her out?
Little Tommy Trout.

What a naughty boy was that
To try to drown poor pussy cat!

Pussy cat, pussy cat,
  where have you been?
I've been to London
  to visit the queen.
Pussy cat, pussy cat,
  what did you there?
I frightened a little mouse
  under her chair.

Humpty-Dumpty sat on a wall,
Humpty-Dumpty had a great fall.
All the king's horses, and all the king's men
Couldn't put Humpty together again.

I SAW A SHIP A-SAILING A-SAILING ON THE SEA

I saw a ship a-sailing,
  A-sailing on the sea,
And oh! it was all laden
  With pretty things for thee!

There were comfits in the cabin,
  And apples in the hold;
The sails were made of silk,
  And the masts were made of gold.

The four-and-twenty sailors
  That stood between the decks
Were four-and-twenty white mice,
  With chains about their necks.

The captain was a duck,
  With a packet on his back;
And when the ship began to move,
  The captain said, "Quack! Quack!"

There was an old woman
Went up in a basket
Ninety times as high as the moon,
And where she was going I could not but ask it
For in her hand she carried a broom.

"Old woman! Old woman, old woman!" said I,
"Whither, oh whither, oh whither so high?"

"To sweep the cobwebs right out of the sky,
And I'll be with you by and by."

The lion and the unicorn
Were fighting for the crown;
The lion beat the unicorn
All around the town.

Some gave them white bread,
Some gave them brown;
Some gave them plum cake,
And sent them out of town.

Hush-a-bye baby on the tree top;
When the wind blows the cradle will rock.

When the bough bends, the cradle will fall,
Down will come baby, bough, cradle and all.

OLD·MOTHER HUBBARD

Old Mother Hubbard,
   She went to the cupboard,
To get her poor dog a bone.
When she got there
   The cupboard was bare,
And so the poor dog had none.

She went to the baker's
 To buy him some bread,
But when she came back
 She thought he was dead.

She went to the undertaker's
 To buy him a coffin,
And when she came back
 The sly dog was laughing.

She went to the draper's
  To buy him some linen,
And when she came back
  The good dog was spinning.

She went to the hosier's
  To buy him some hose,
And when she came back
  He was dressed in his clothes.

She went to the hatter's
  To buy him a hat,
And when she came back
  He was feeding the cat.

She went to the tailor's
  To buy him a coat,
And when she came home
  He was riding the goat.

She went to the barber's
  To buy him a wig,
And when she came back
  He was dancing a jig.

She went to the butcher's
To get him some tripe,
And when she came back
He was smoking a pipe.

She went to the fish shop
To buy him some fish,
And when she came back
He was washing the dish.

The dame made a curtsy,
The dog made a bow;
The dame said, "Your servant,"
The dog said, "Bow-wow."

Rock-a-bye, baby,
thy cradle is green;
Father's a nobleman,
Mother's a queen;
And Betty's a lady,
and wears a gold ring;
And Johnny's a drummer,
and drums for the king.

Jack and Jill went up the hill,
To fetch a pail of water;

Jack fell down and broke his crown,
And Jill came tumbling after.

I HAD A LITTLE HEN

I had a little hen;
The prettiest ever seen;
She washed me the dishes,
And kept the house clean;

She went to the mill
To fetch me some flour;
She brought it home
In less than an hour.

She baked me my bread,
She brew'd me my ale,
She sat by the fire
And told many a fine tale.

Deedle, deedle, dumpling, my son John,
Went to bed with his trousers on;
One shoe off, and one shoe on,
Deedle, deedle, dumpling, my son John.

Wee Willie Winkie
   Runs through the town,
Upstairs and downstairs,
   In his nightgown.
Rapping at the window,
   Crying through the lock,
"Are the children all in bed?
   For it's past eight o'clock."

The man in the moon
     looked out of the moon,
Looked out of the moon and said,
" 'Tis time for all the children
     on the earth
To think about going to bed!"

THE
END . .